Lacy Sunshine's Pretty Parcels and Sunshine Dreamers Coloring Book Volume 30

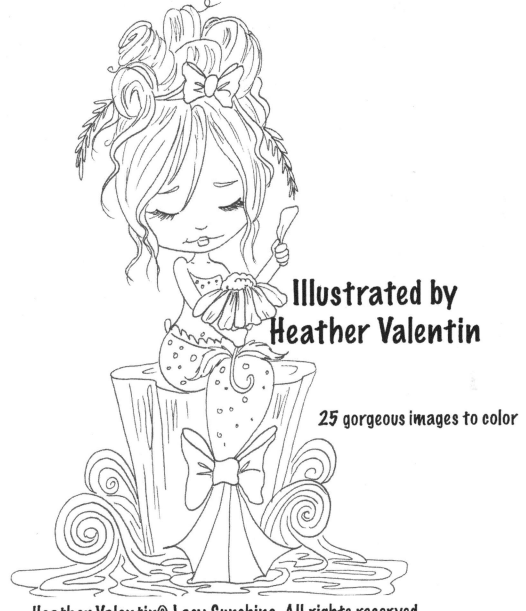

Illustrated by Heather Valentin

25 gorgeous images to color

MW01201022

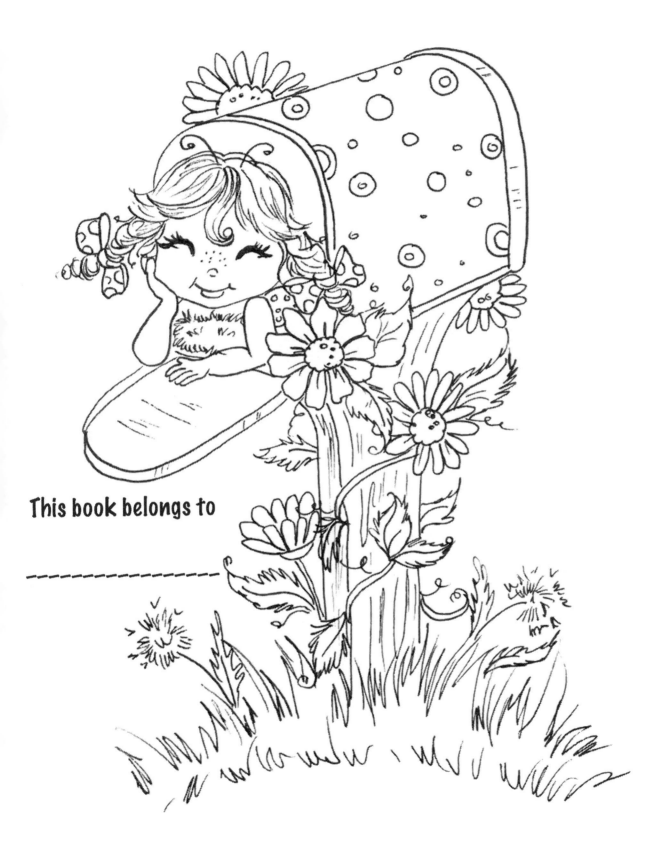

This book belongs to

_____

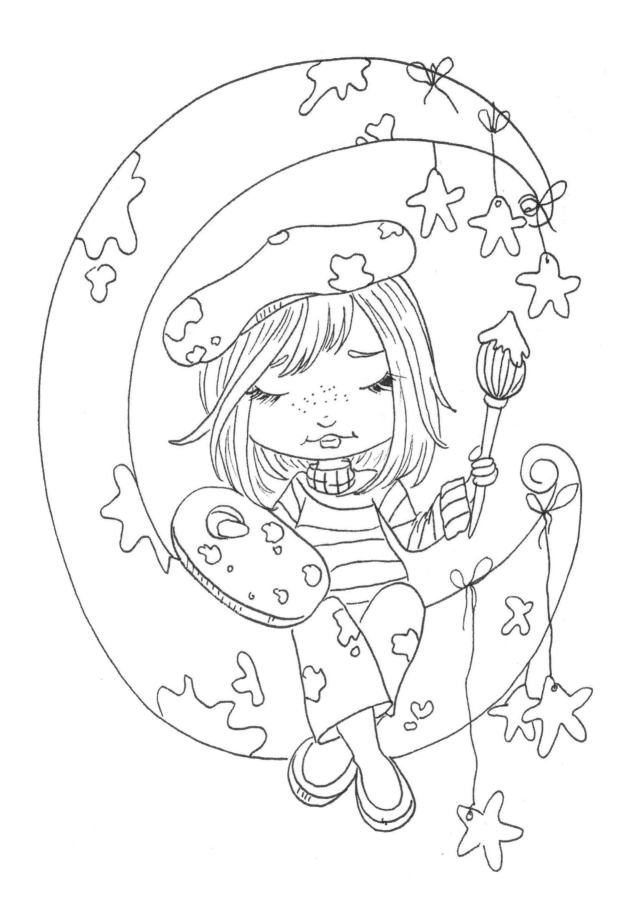

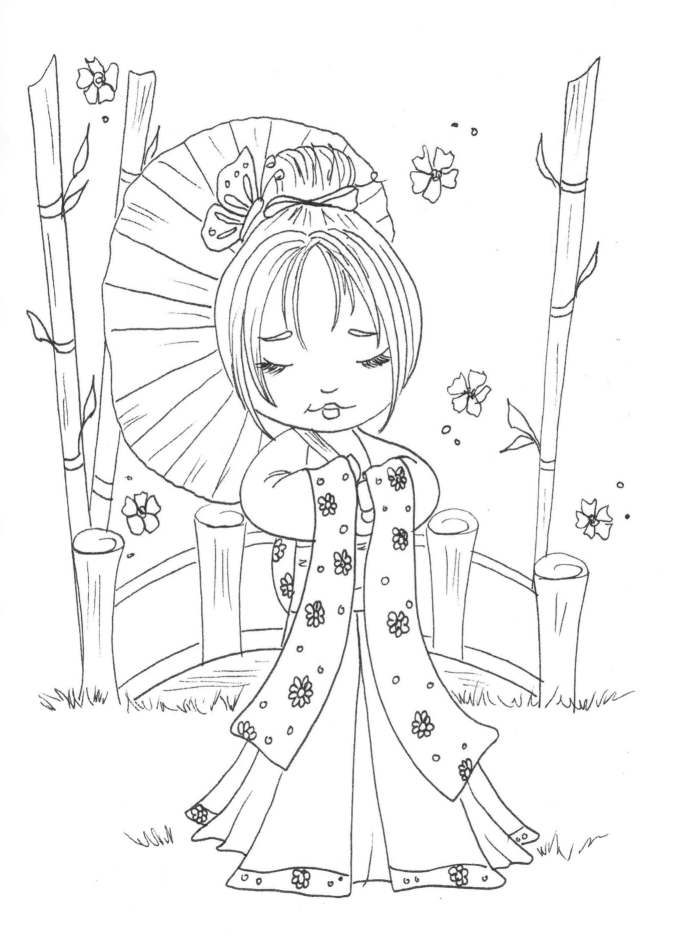

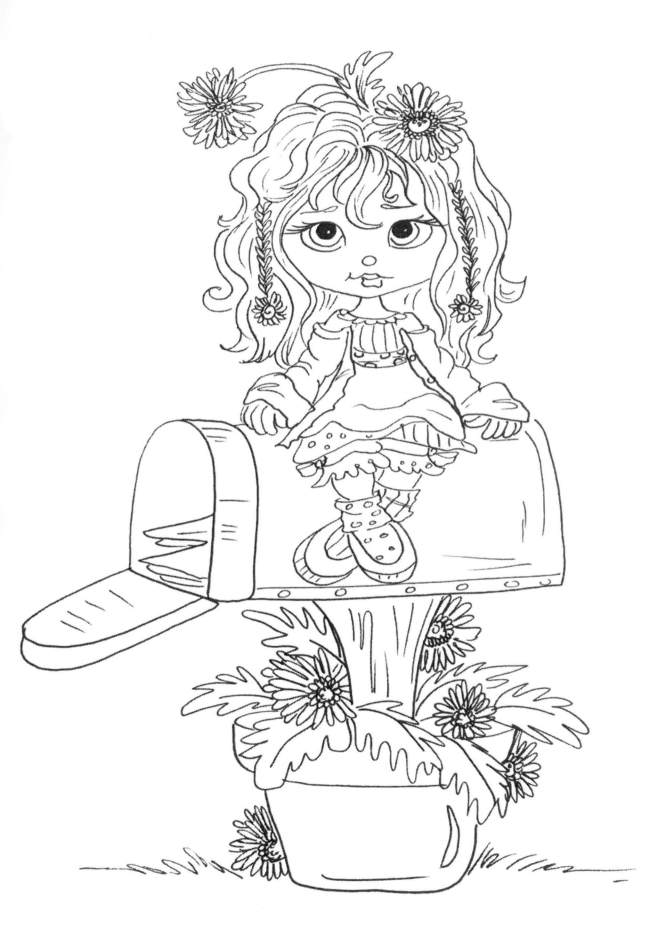

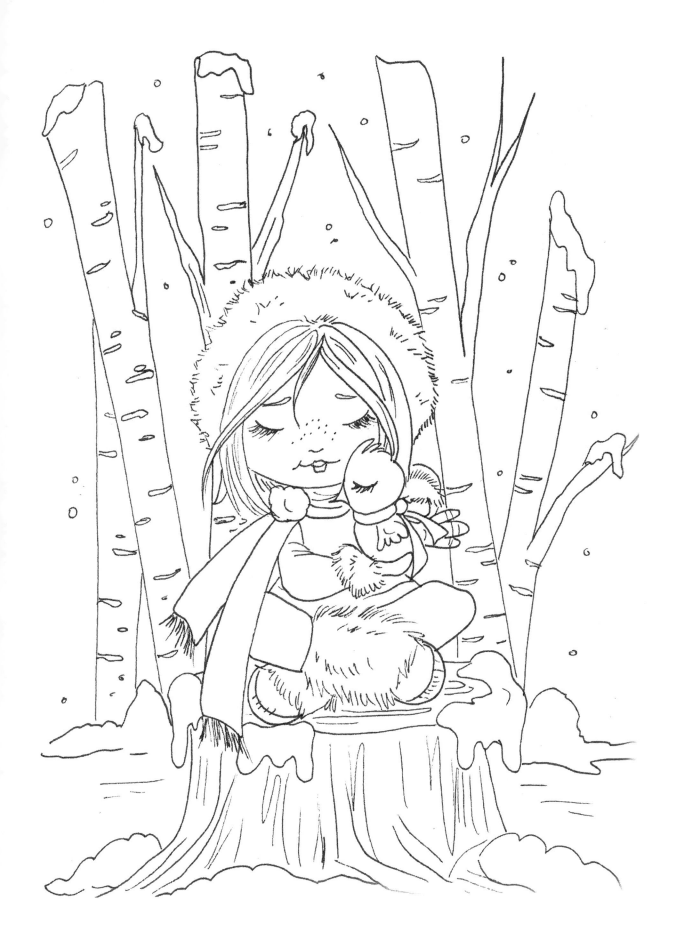

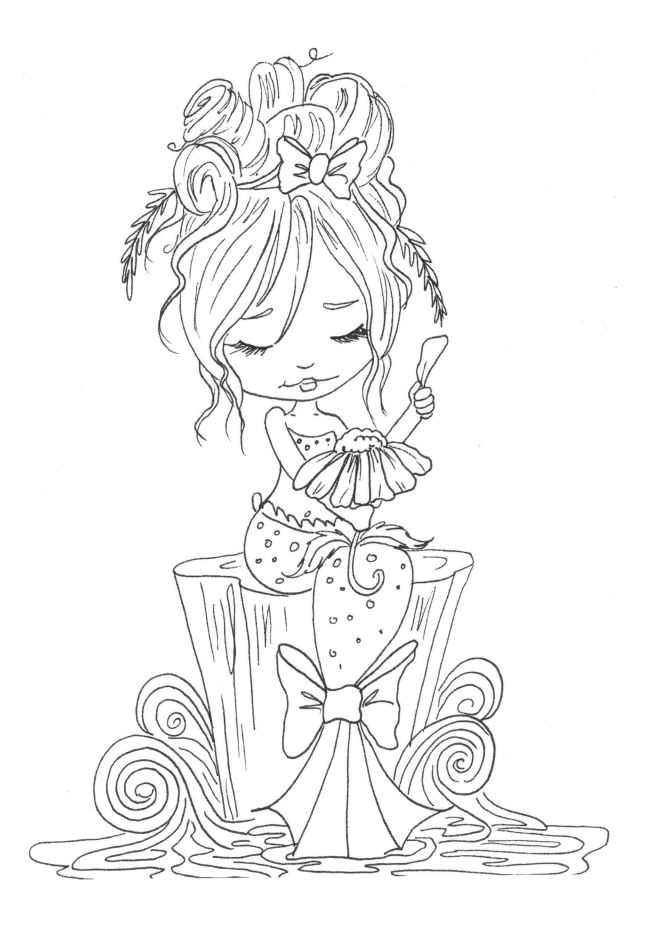

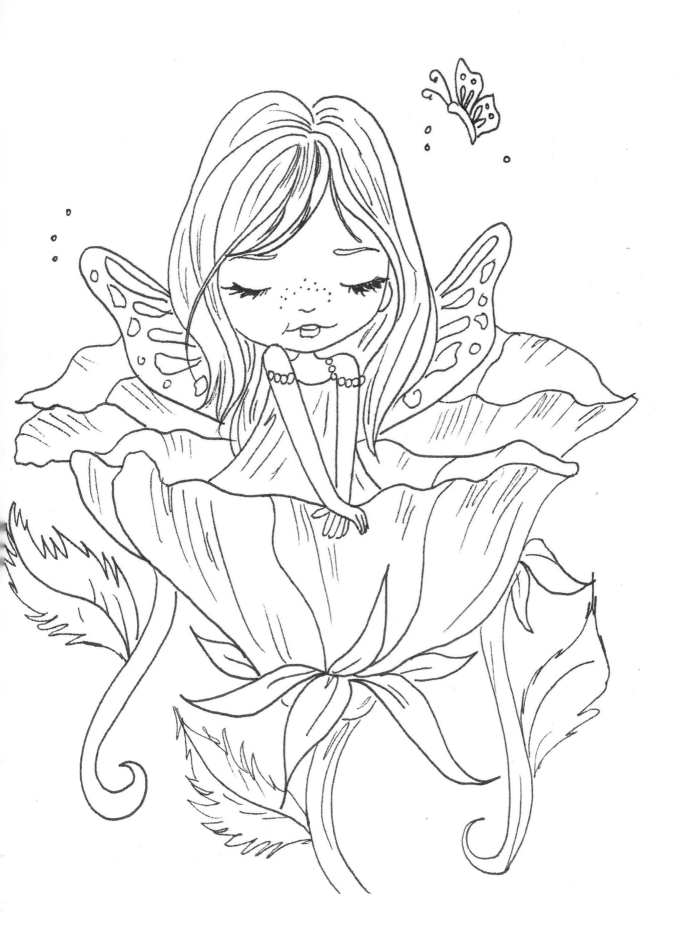

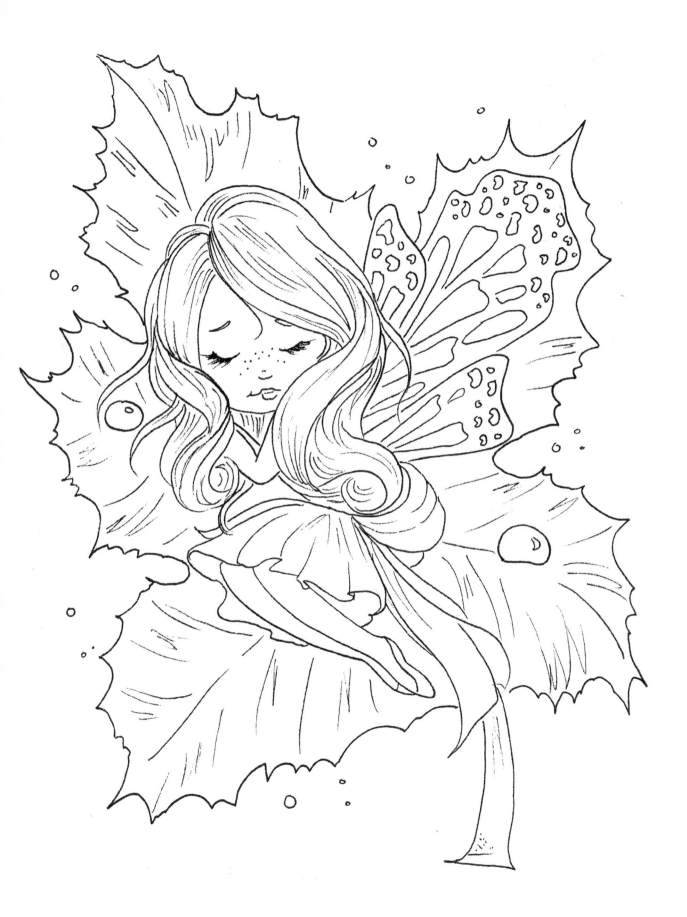

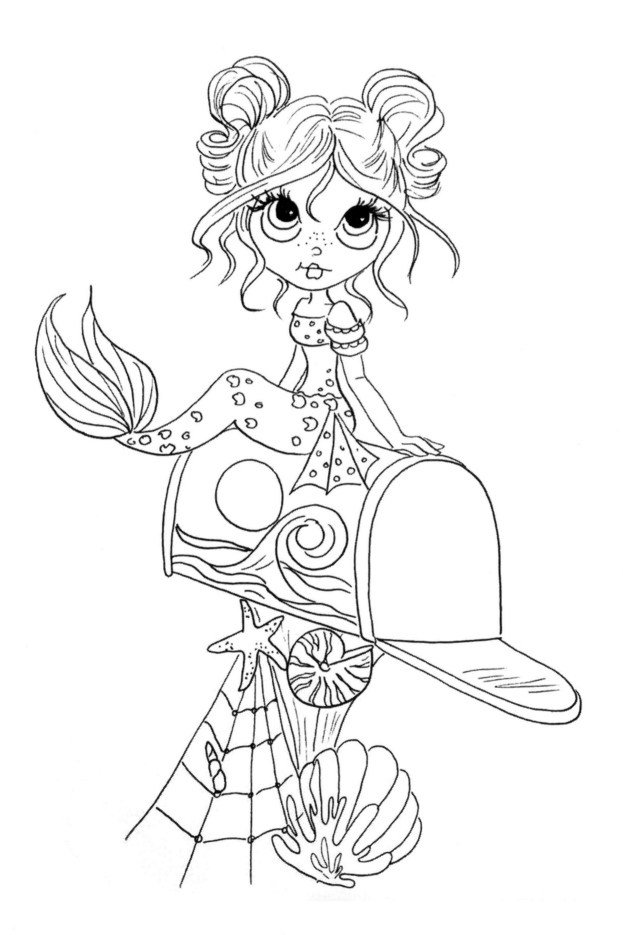

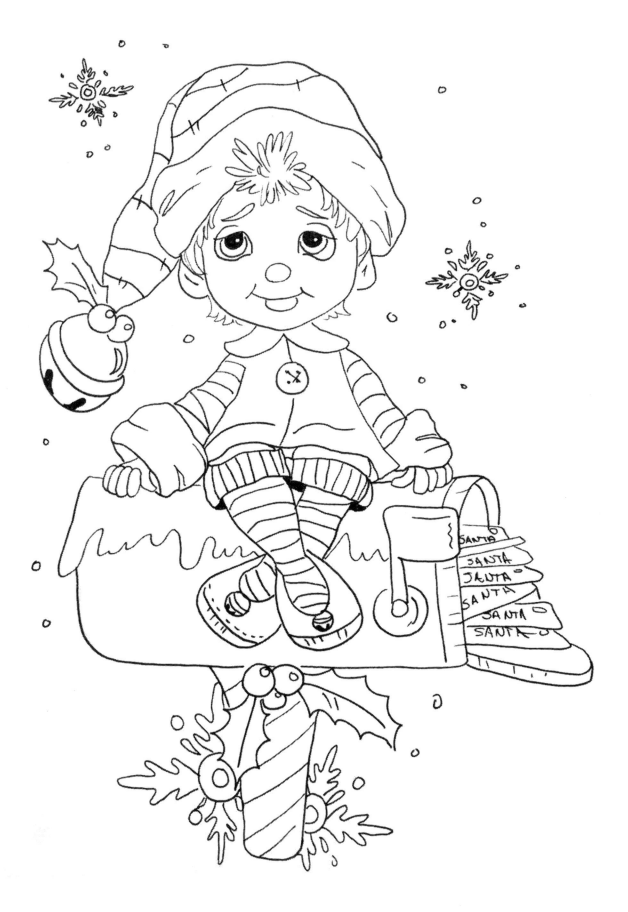

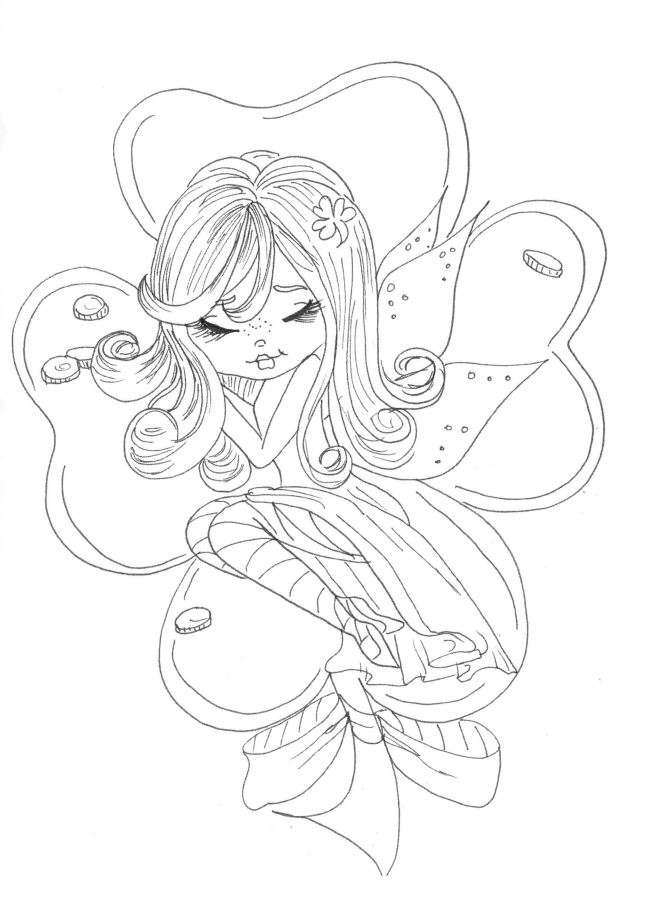

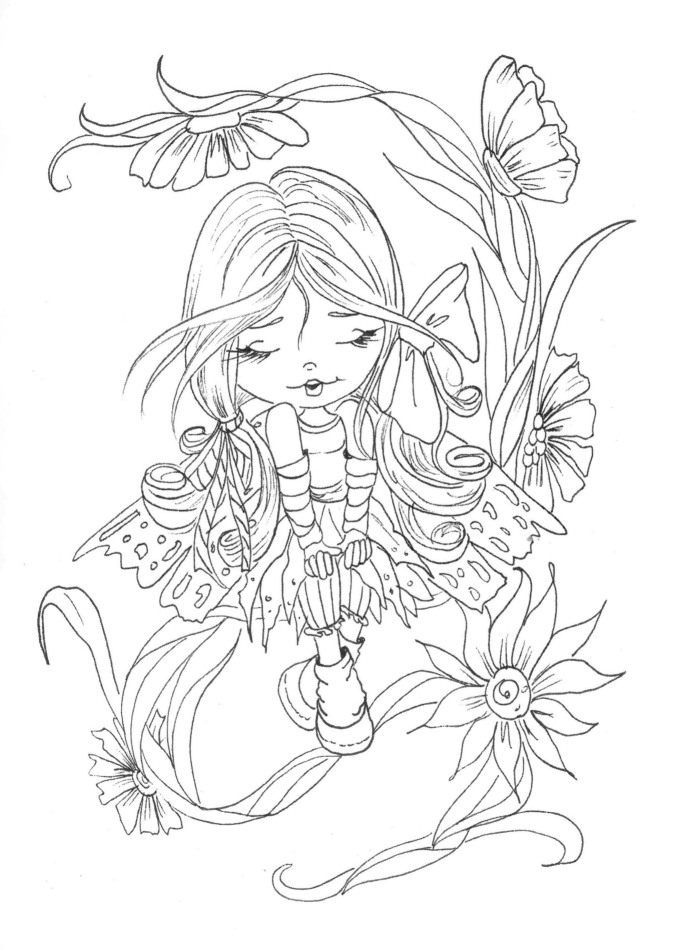

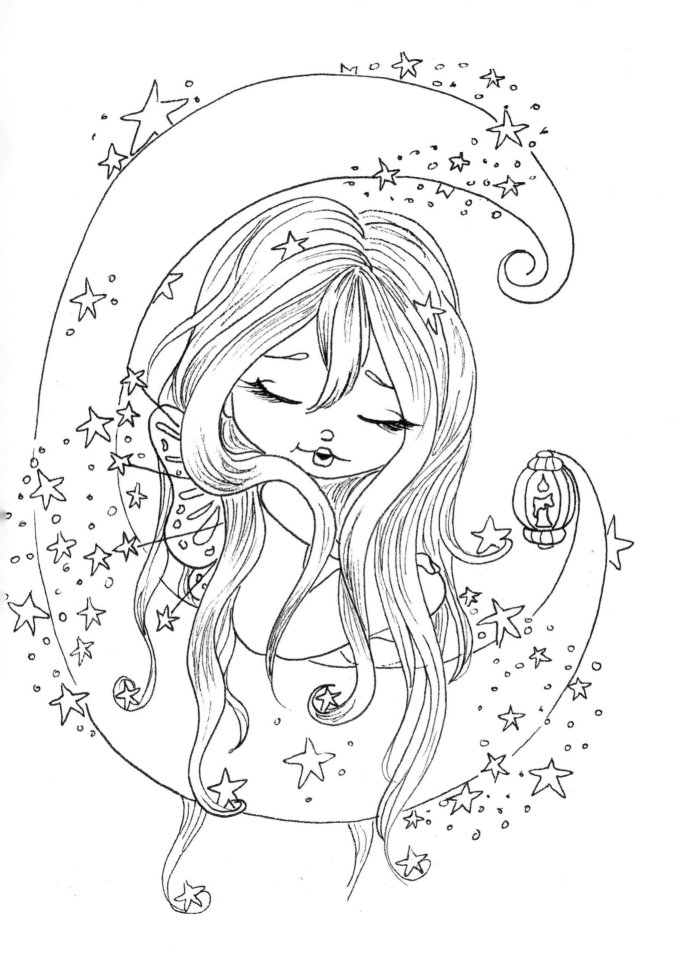

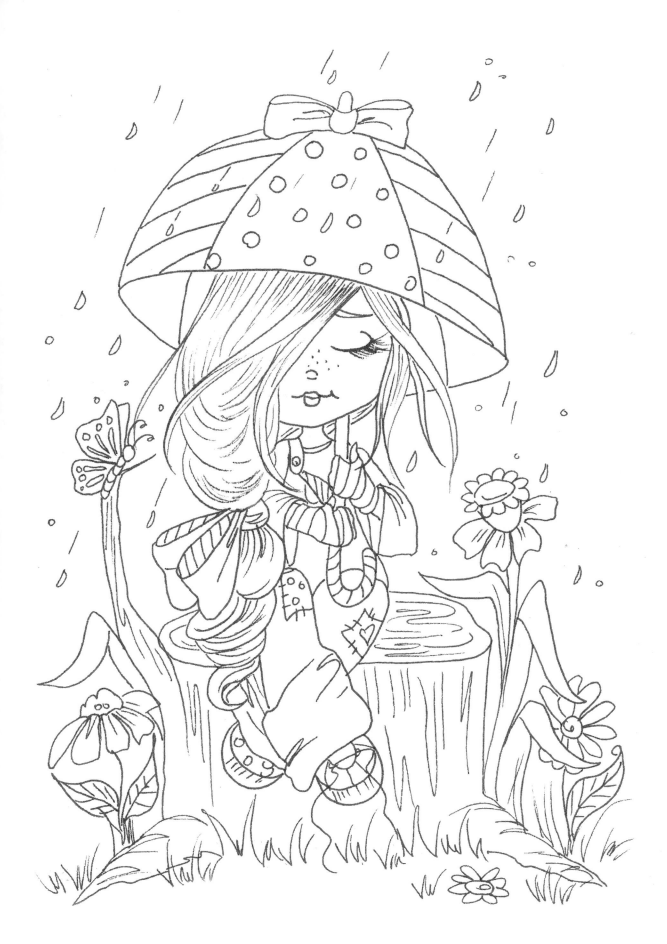

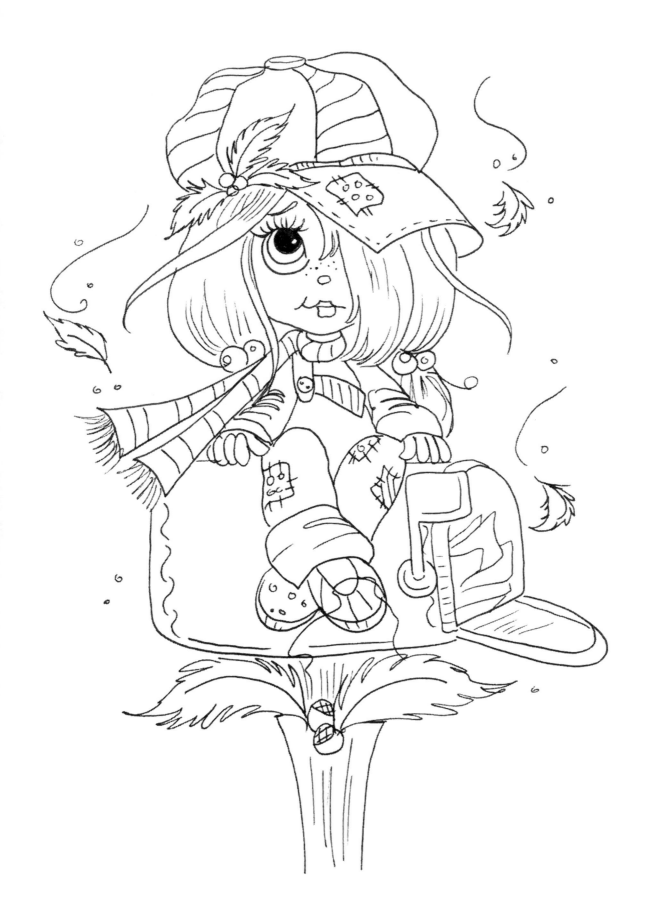

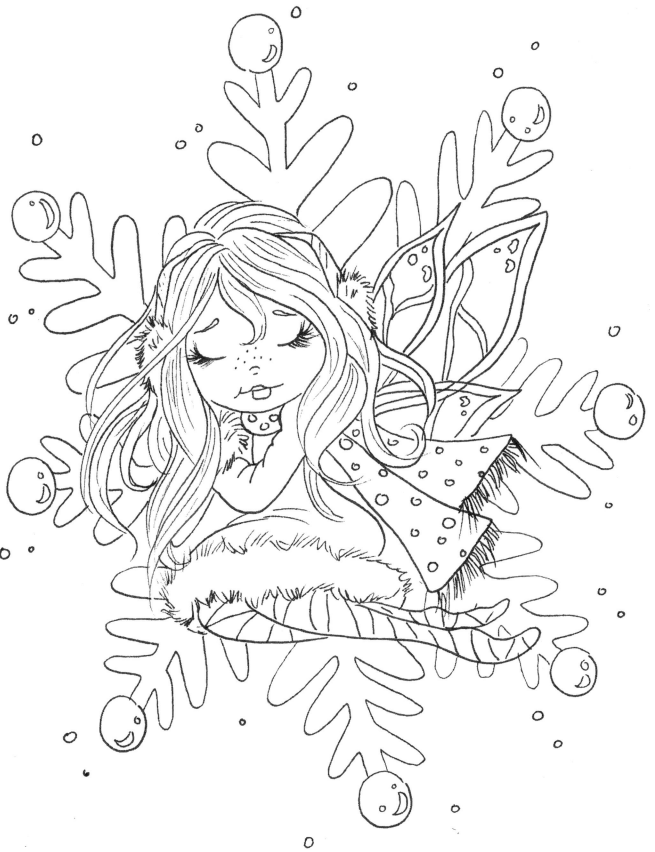

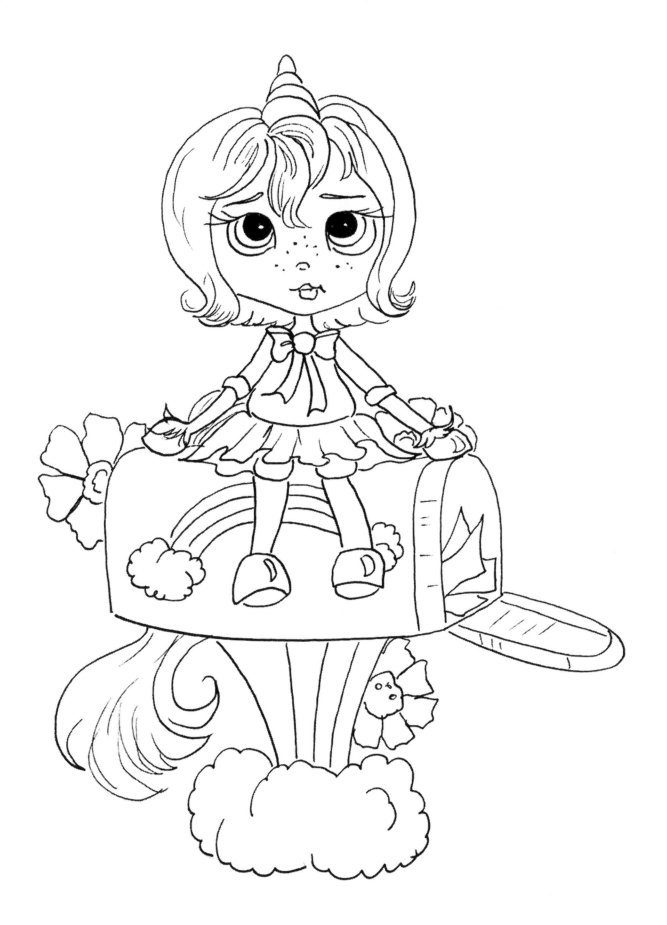

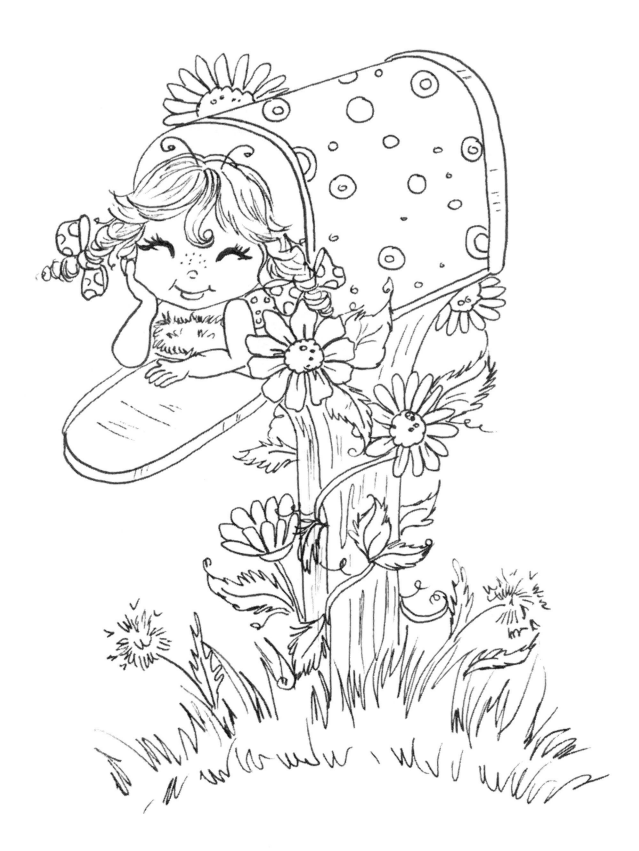

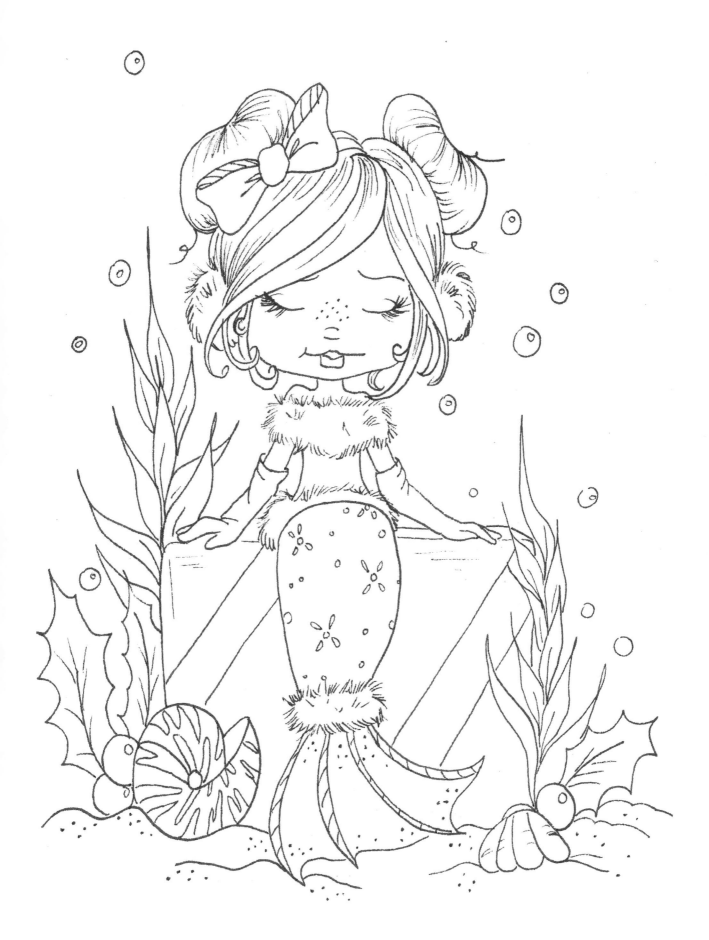

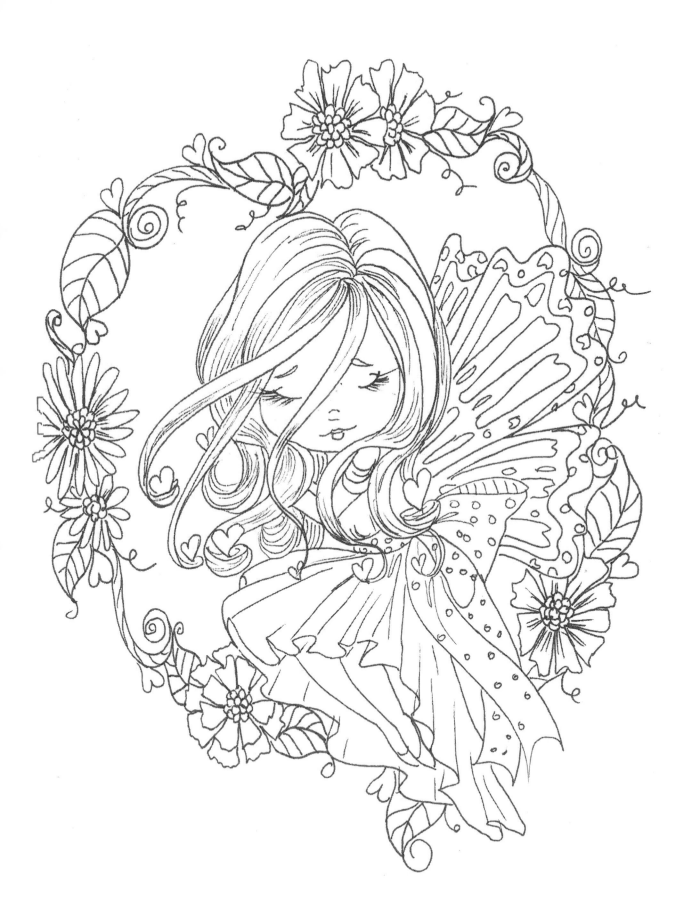

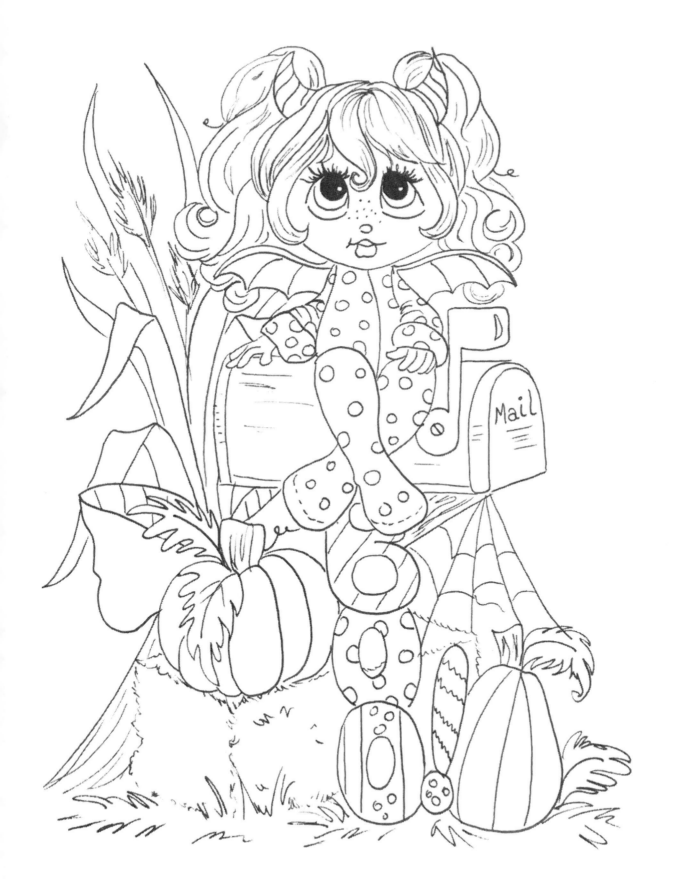

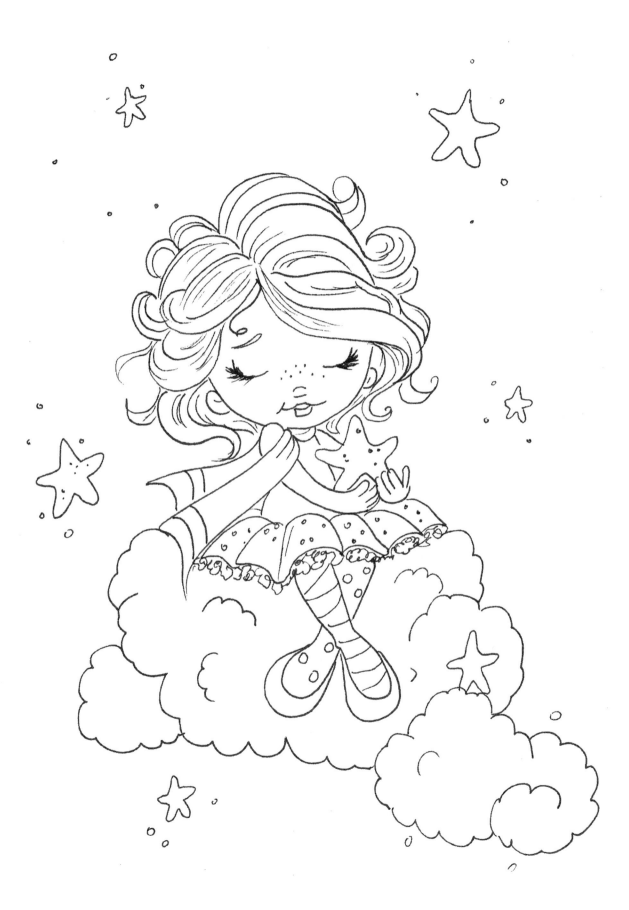

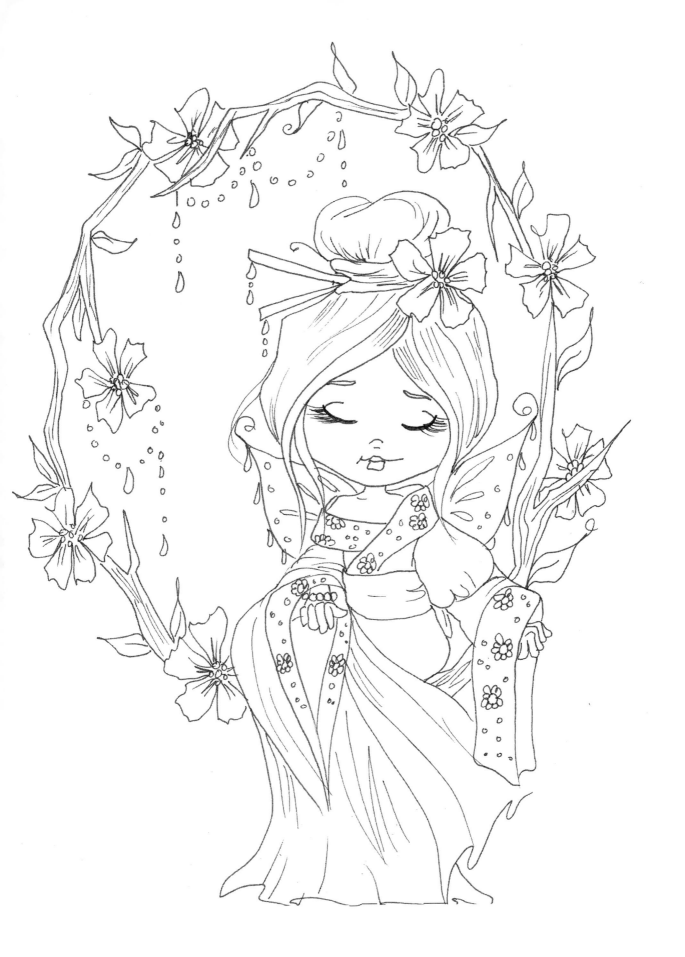

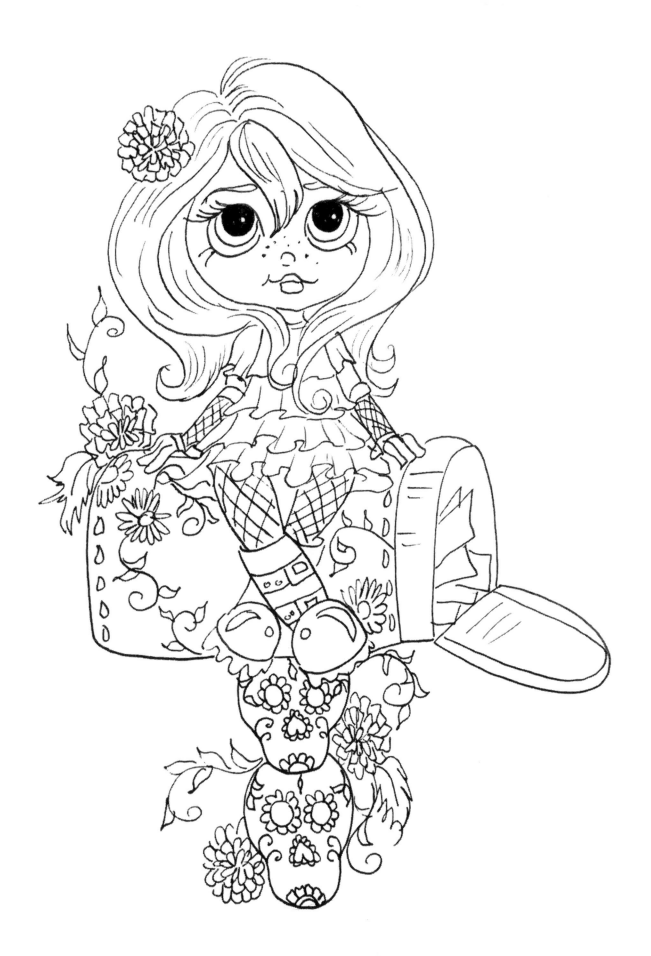

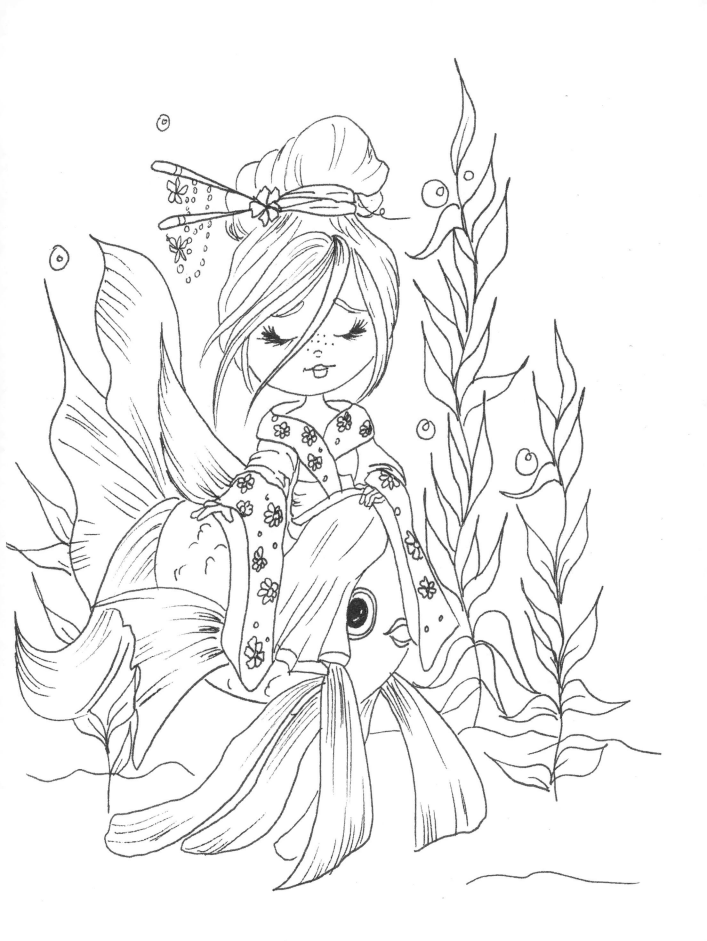

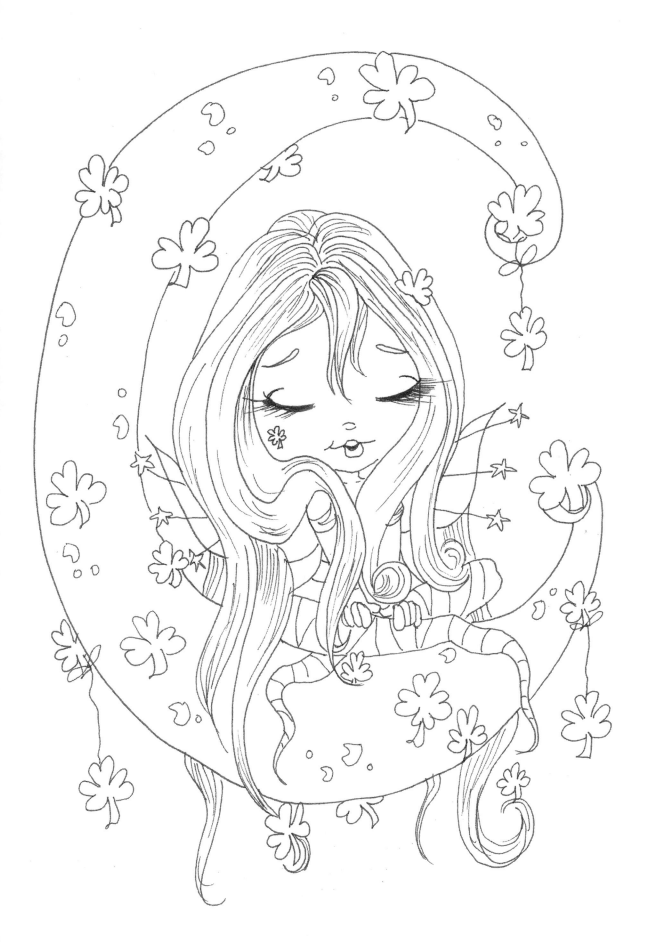

Made in the USA
San Bernardino, CA
21 November 2018